動物的適應性

Sharing the Planet | Non-Fiction Series

Copyright © 2022 by Level Learning, INC. and Washington Yu Ying PCS™
Original and Edited Text Copyright © 2022 by Washington Yu Ying PCS™

All rights reserved. No part of this book in whole or part may be reproduced without written permission from the publisher.

Published by Level Learning, INC.
Content Contributors:
Washington Yu Ying PCS™ - Jianhua (Allen) Zhong, Pearl Zao He You
Level Learning - Jingyao Qi

Illustrations by: Josh Taira

Leveling classification based on Level Learning standard.
For full description, visit www.levellearning.com

ISBN 978-1-64040-064-1
Traditional Chinese Edition

About Level Learning:
Level Learning provides a literacy focused curriculum specifically designed for K-12 Chinese as a Second Language classrooms. Our program offers 20 levels of specific and detailed objectives, leveled texts and passages, mastery-based online assessment, and analytics to enable data-driven instruction. Level Learning reading curriculum for both literature and informational text emphasize grammar and comprehension skills to help teachers develop confident and independent Chinese language readers. The non-fiction series of books are specifically designed to support our informational text course based on multiple national standards. To learn more about our entire offering, visit www.levellearning.com

About Washington Yu Ying PCS™:
Washington Yu Ying PCS is a Mandarin English dual language immersion International Baccalaureate (IB) World school. Yu Ying's mission is to inspire and prepare young people to create a better world by challenging them to reach their full potential in a nurturing Chinese/English educational environment. Yu Ying's comprehensive IB, dual immersion curriculum equips students with global competencies for success in the real world. As a leader in immersion education, Yu Ying is determined to advance Chinese language programs and global citizenry education by helping other schools create and strengthen their Chinese programs. For more information, email: products@washingtonyuying.org

長頸鹿有長長的脖子。
牠可以吃到高處的樹葉。

北極熊有厚厚的皮毛。
牠不怕寒冷的冬天。

蚱蜢為什麼是綠色的？綠色的草可以保護綠色的蚱蜢。

袋鼠媽媽為什麼有個袋子？溫暖的袋子可以保護袋鼠寶寶。

這是動物的適應性。適應性可以幫助動物生存。

Glossary

	Pinyin	English Definition
長頸鹿	cháng jǐng lù	giraffe
脖子	bó zi	neck
可以	kě yǐ	can
北極熊	běi jí xióng	polar bear
厚	hòu	thick
皮毛	pí máo	skin and fur
蚱蜢	zhà měng	grasshopper
保護	bǎo hù	to protect
袋鼠	dài shǔ	kangaroo
袋	dài	(kangaroo's) pouch
溫暖	wēn nuǎn	warm
動物	dòng wù	animal
適應性	shì yìng xìng	adaptability
幫助	bāng zhù	to help
生存	shēng cún	to survive

www.ingramcontent.com/pod-product-compliance
Lightning Source LLC
Chambersburg PA
CBHW041227070526

44584CB00001B/123